Smoky Mountain Wildflowers

Adult Coloring Book

Dale McSwain

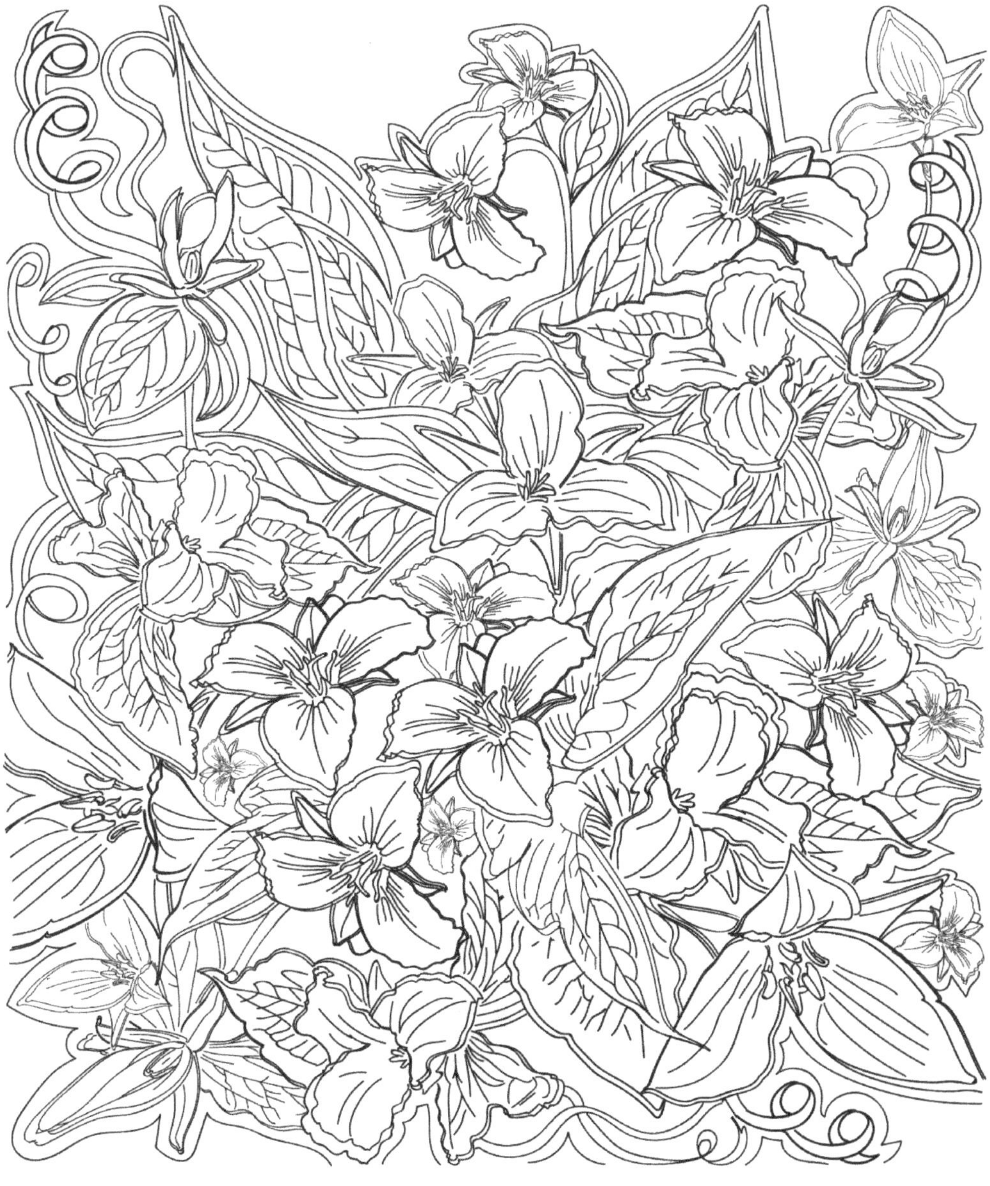

ISBN: 1523336714
ISBN-13: 978-1523336715

For
Sherrie, Sarah, Jeramie and Aubrie

Consider how the wild flowers grow. They do not labor or spin.
Yet I tell you not even Solomon in all his splendor was dressed as one of these.
Luke 12:27

stelleriabooks.com
Visit our website for wildflower photographs and discounts on future publications.

CONTENTS

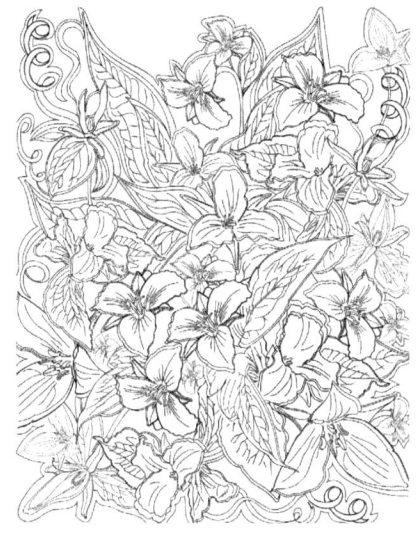

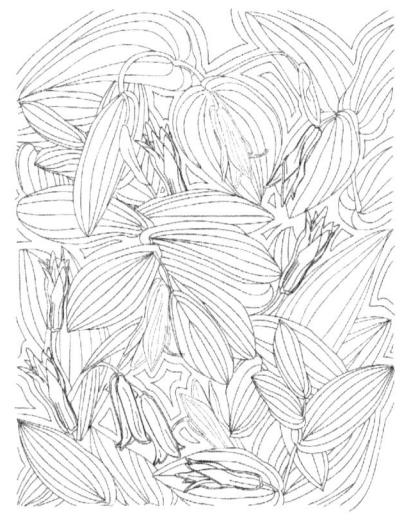
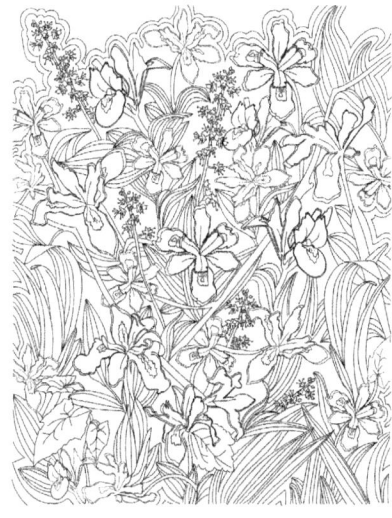

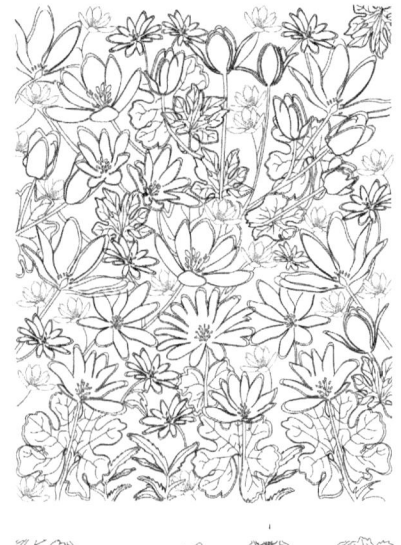

Bloodroot

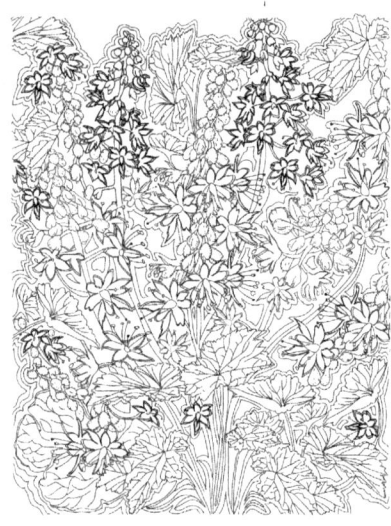

Foamflower

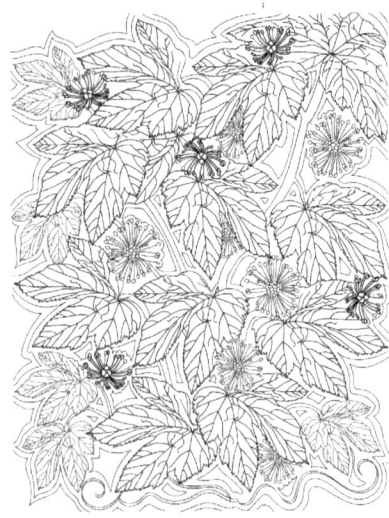

Goldenseal

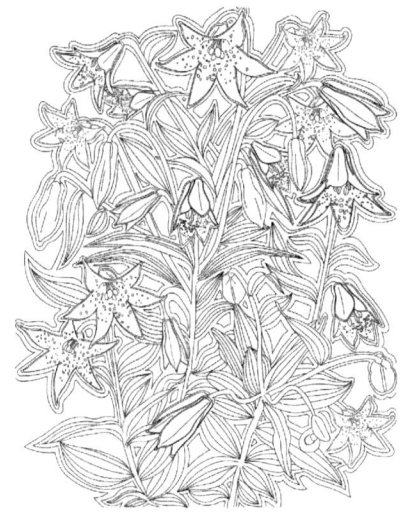

Grays Lily

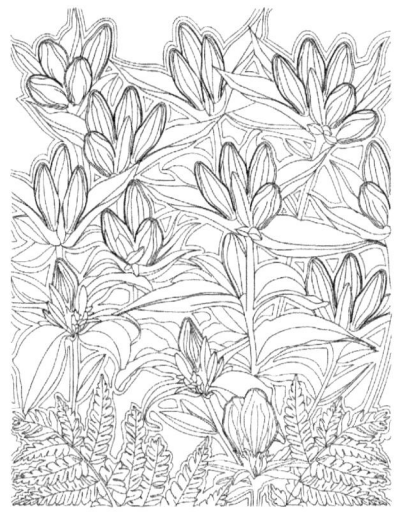

Closed Gentian

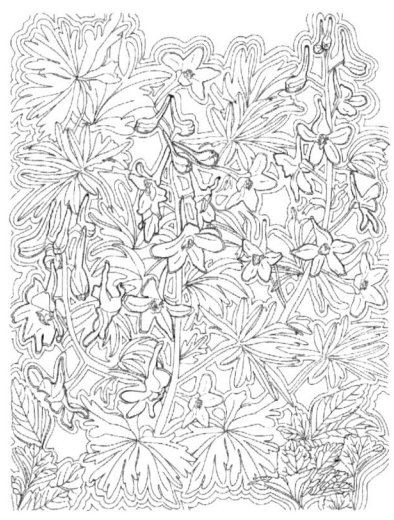

Larkspur

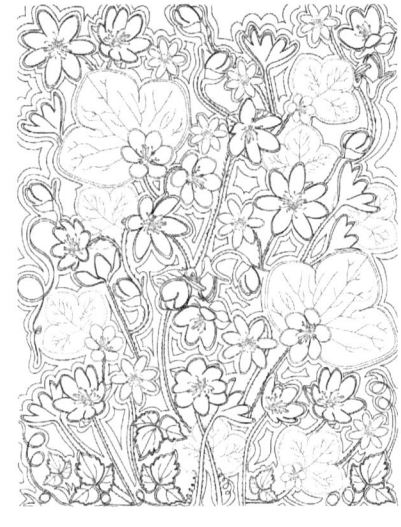

Hepetica

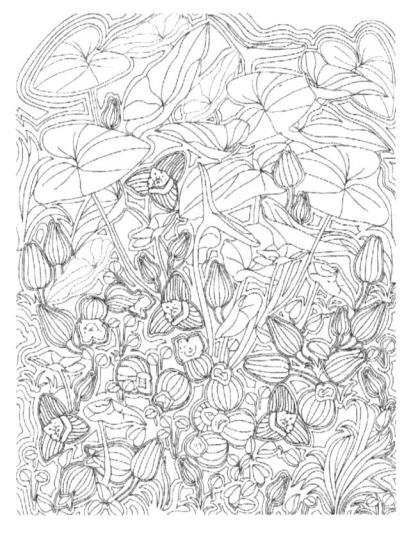

Lil Brown Jug

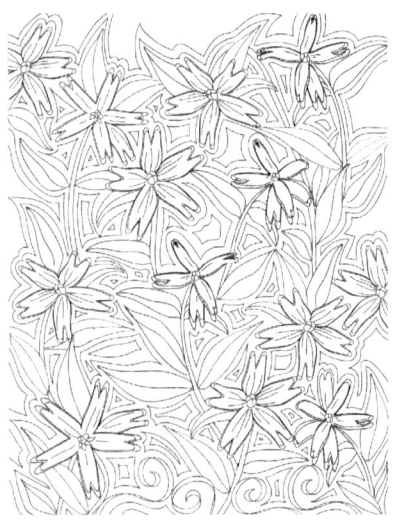

Firepink

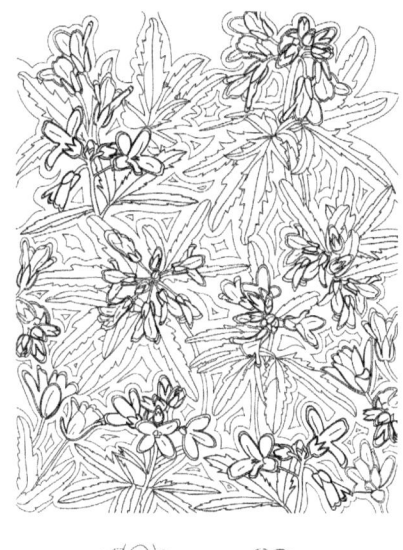

Toothwort

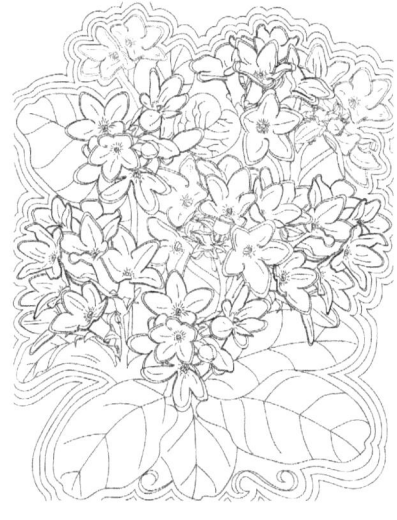

Trailing Arbutus

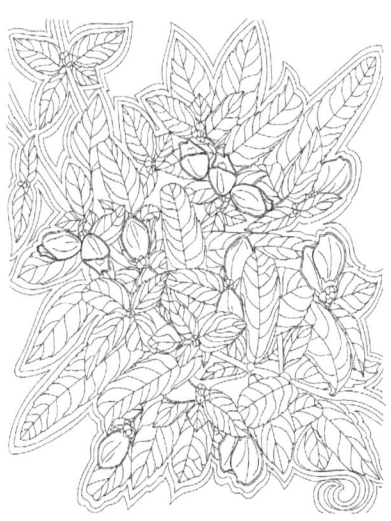

Turtlehead

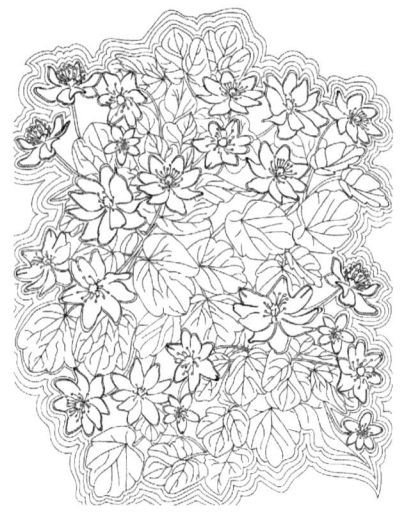

Rue Anemone

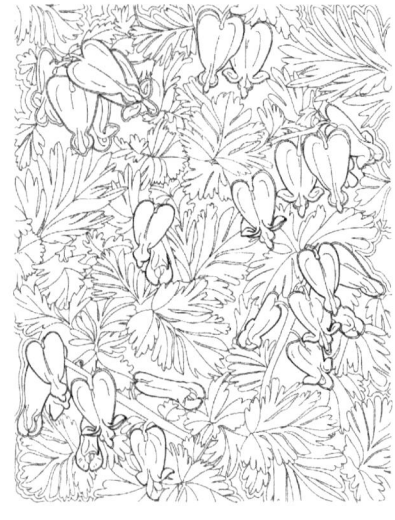

Squirrel Corn

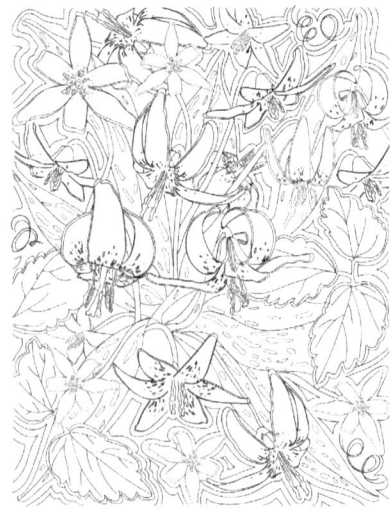

Trout Lily

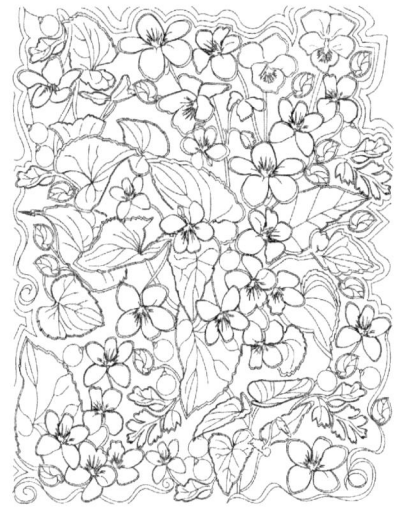

Violet

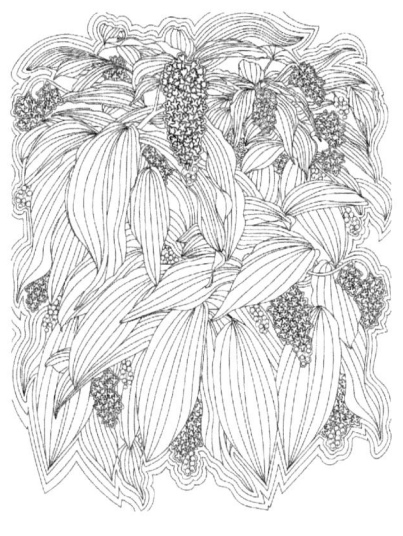

False Solomon's Seal

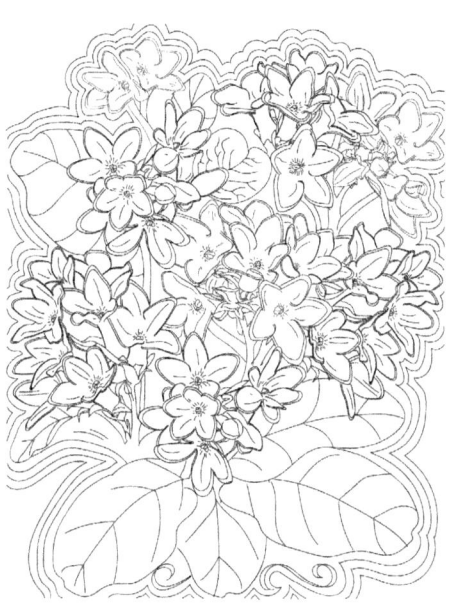

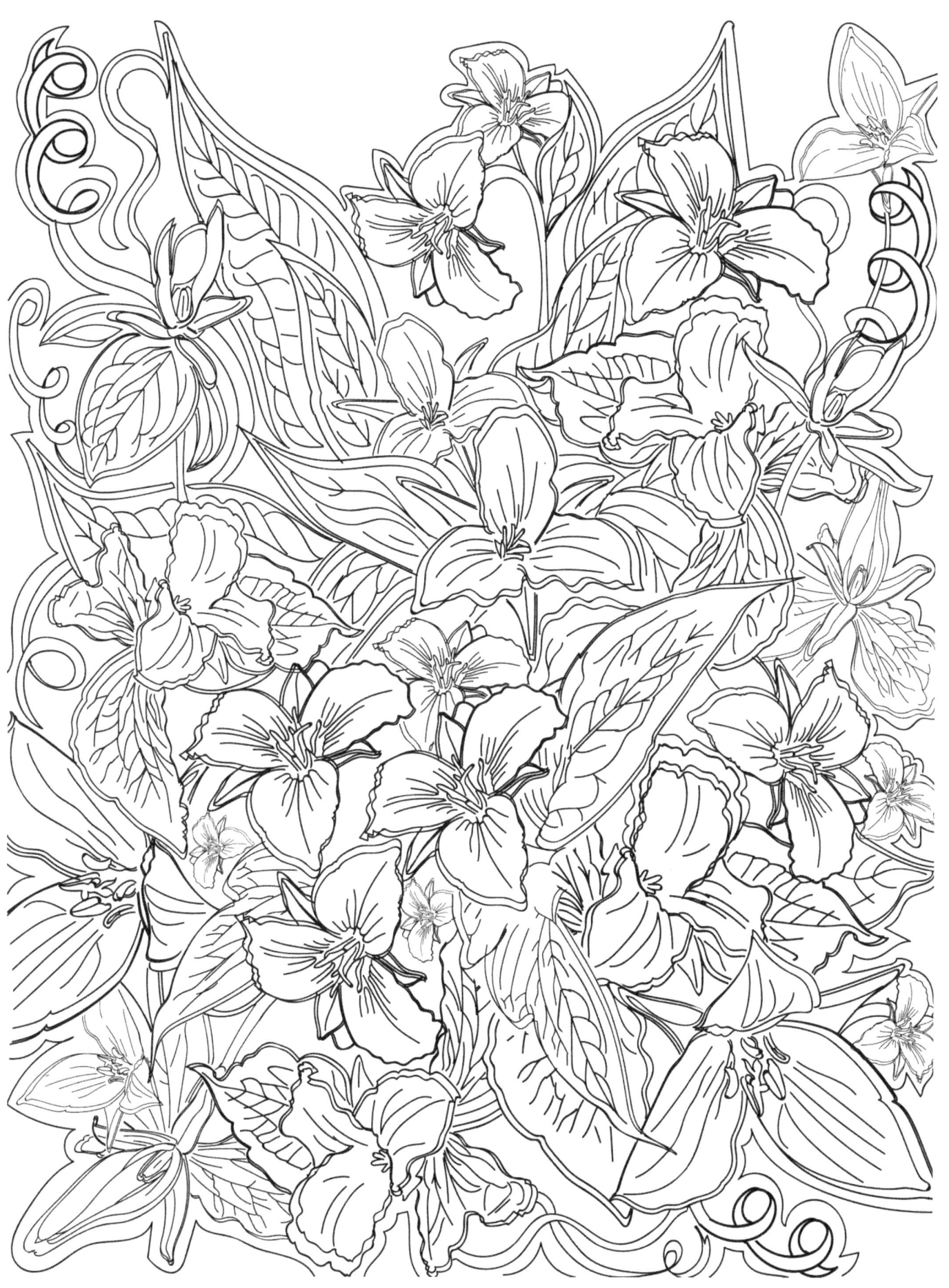

Trillium

Artwork By:

Completed On:

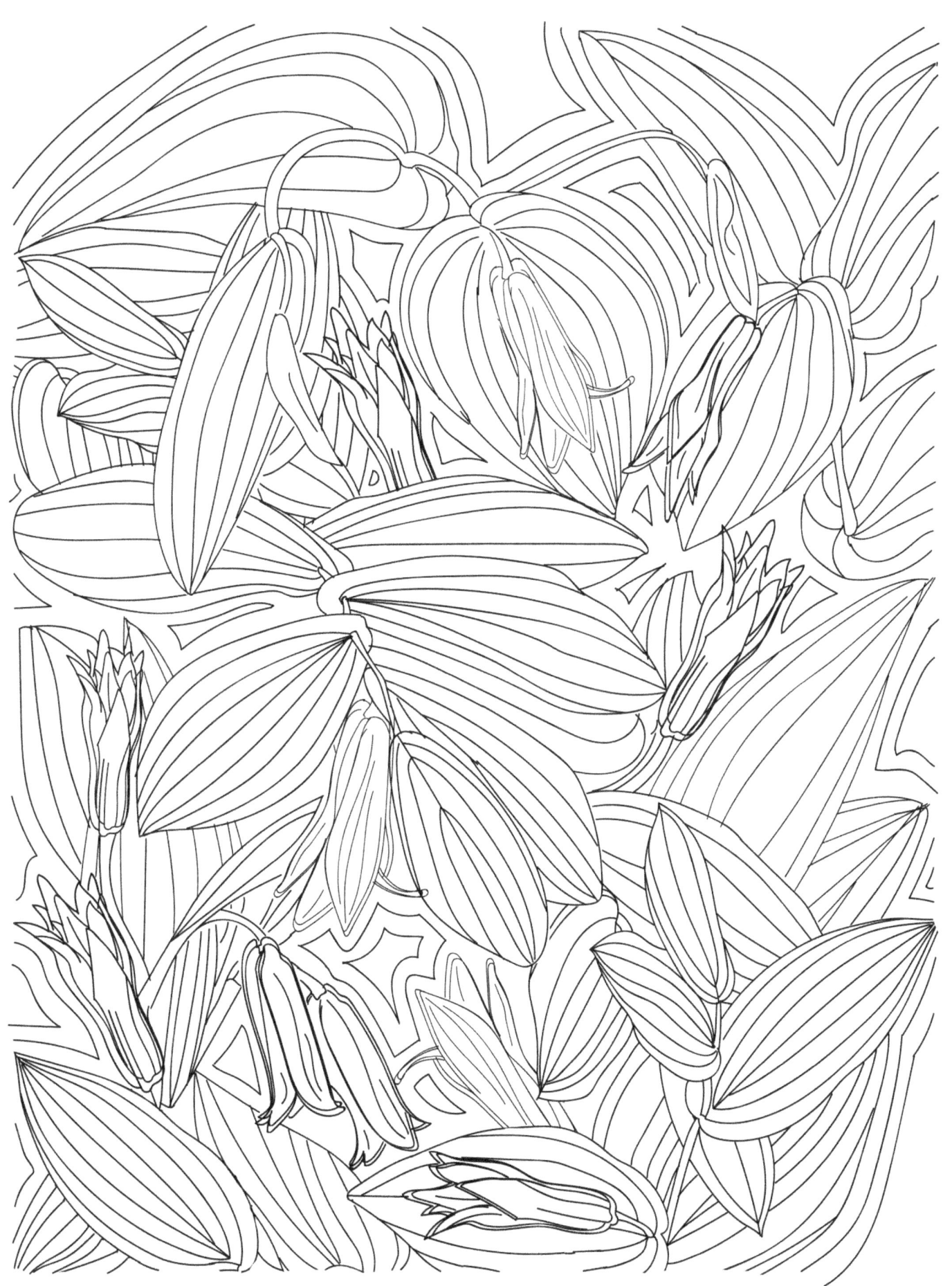

Bellwort

Artwork By:

Completed On:

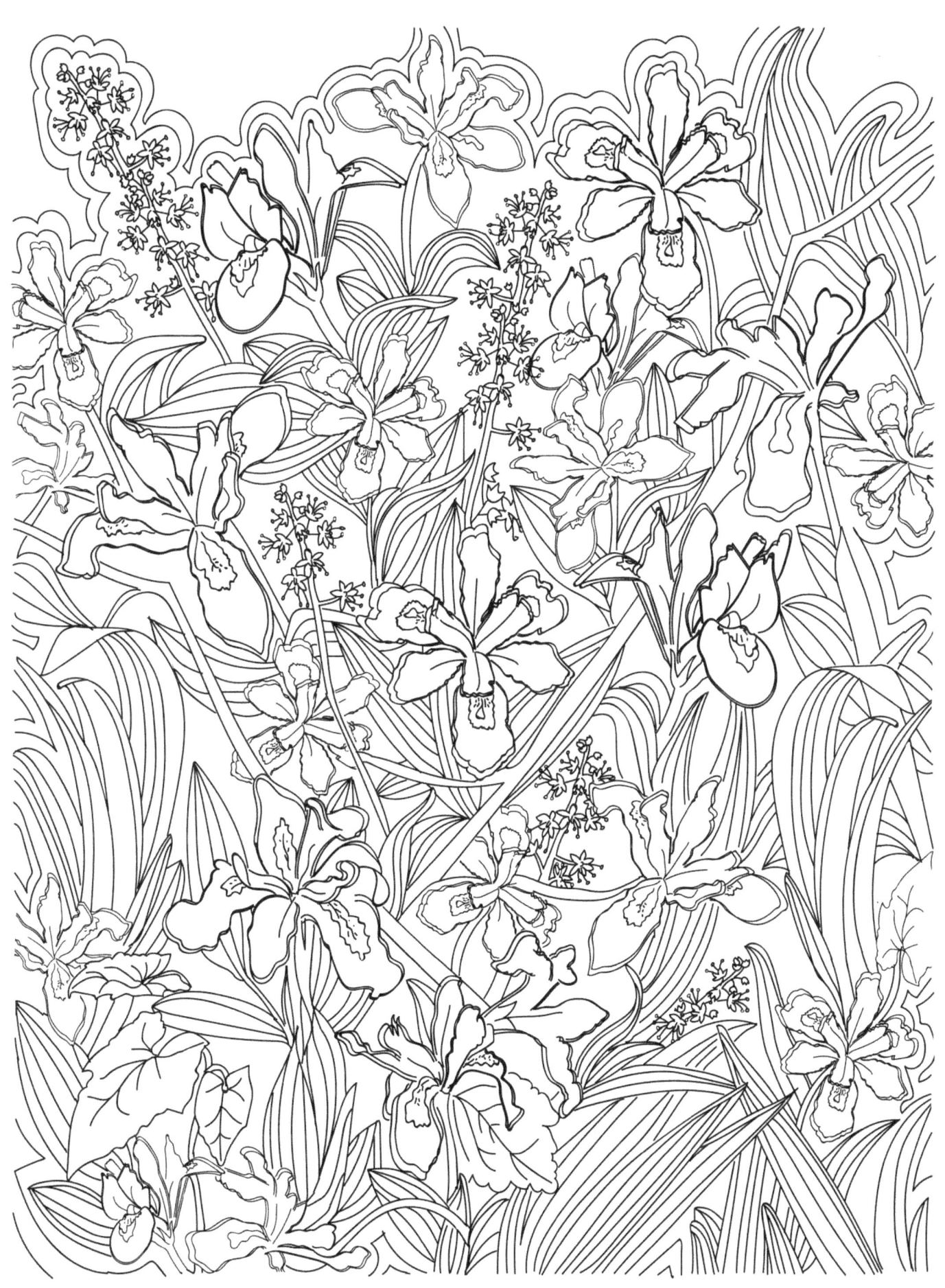

Dwarf Iris

Artwork By:

Completed On:

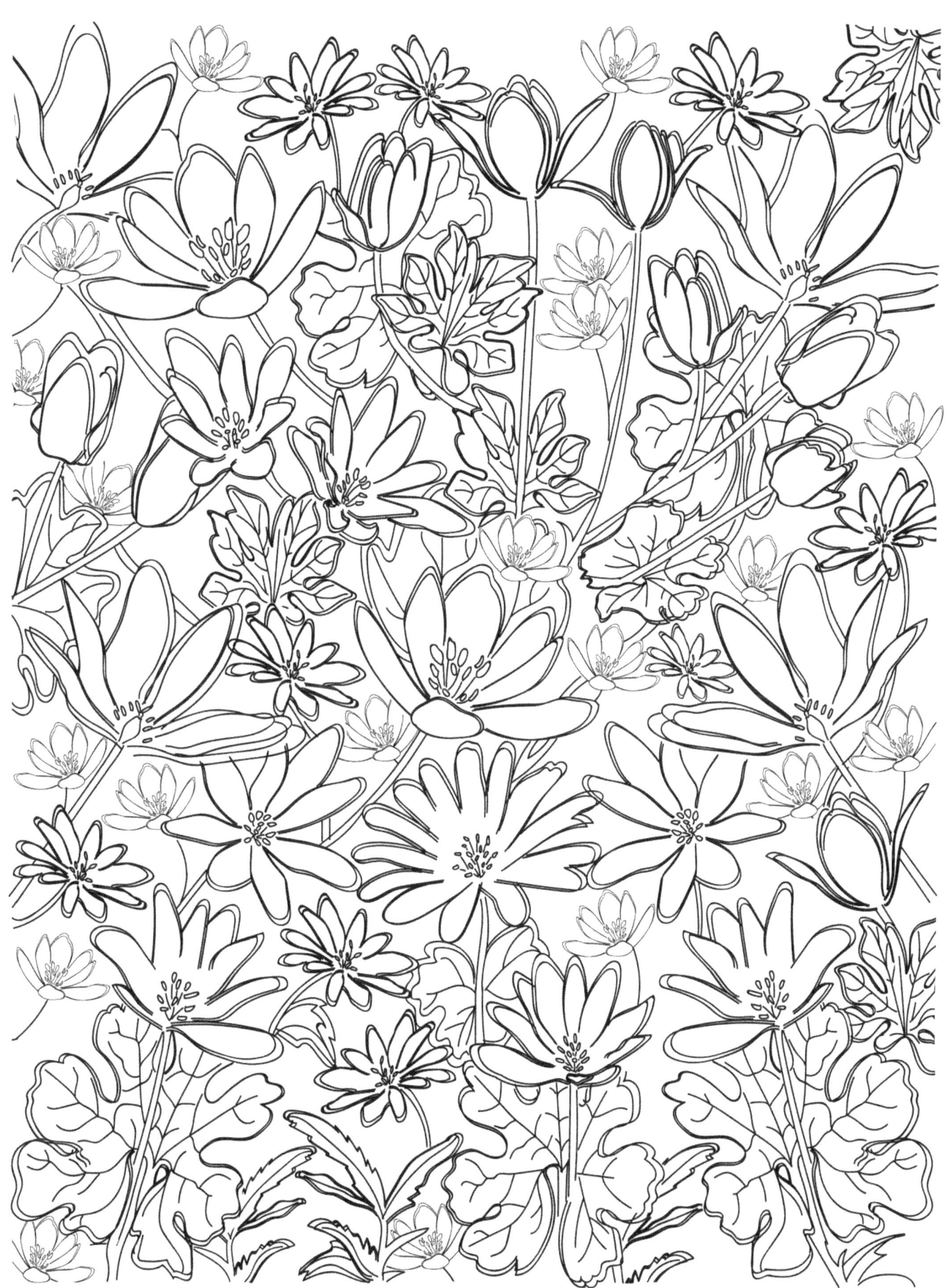

Bloodroot

Artwork By:

Completed On:

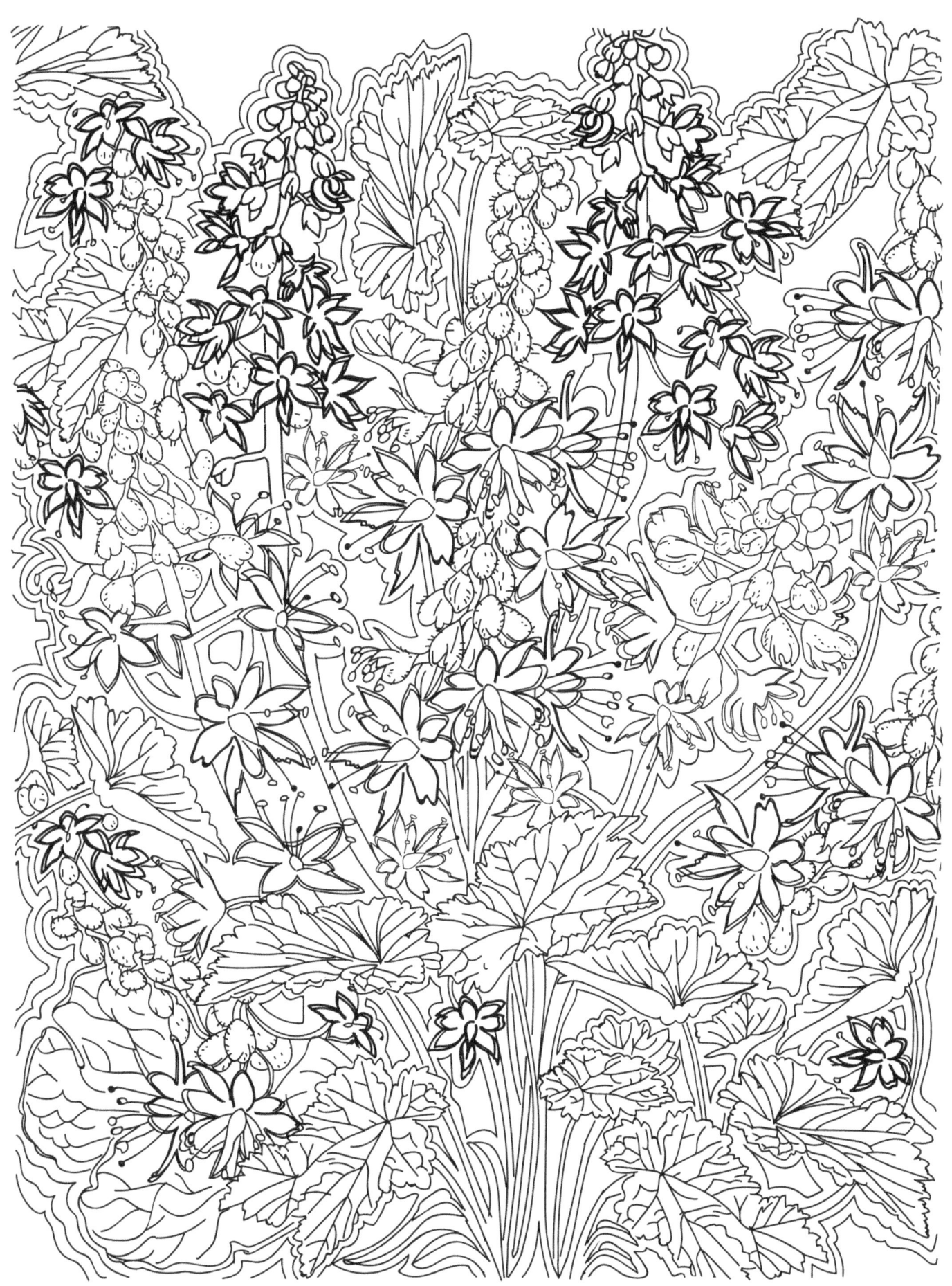

Foamflower

Artwork By:

Completed On:

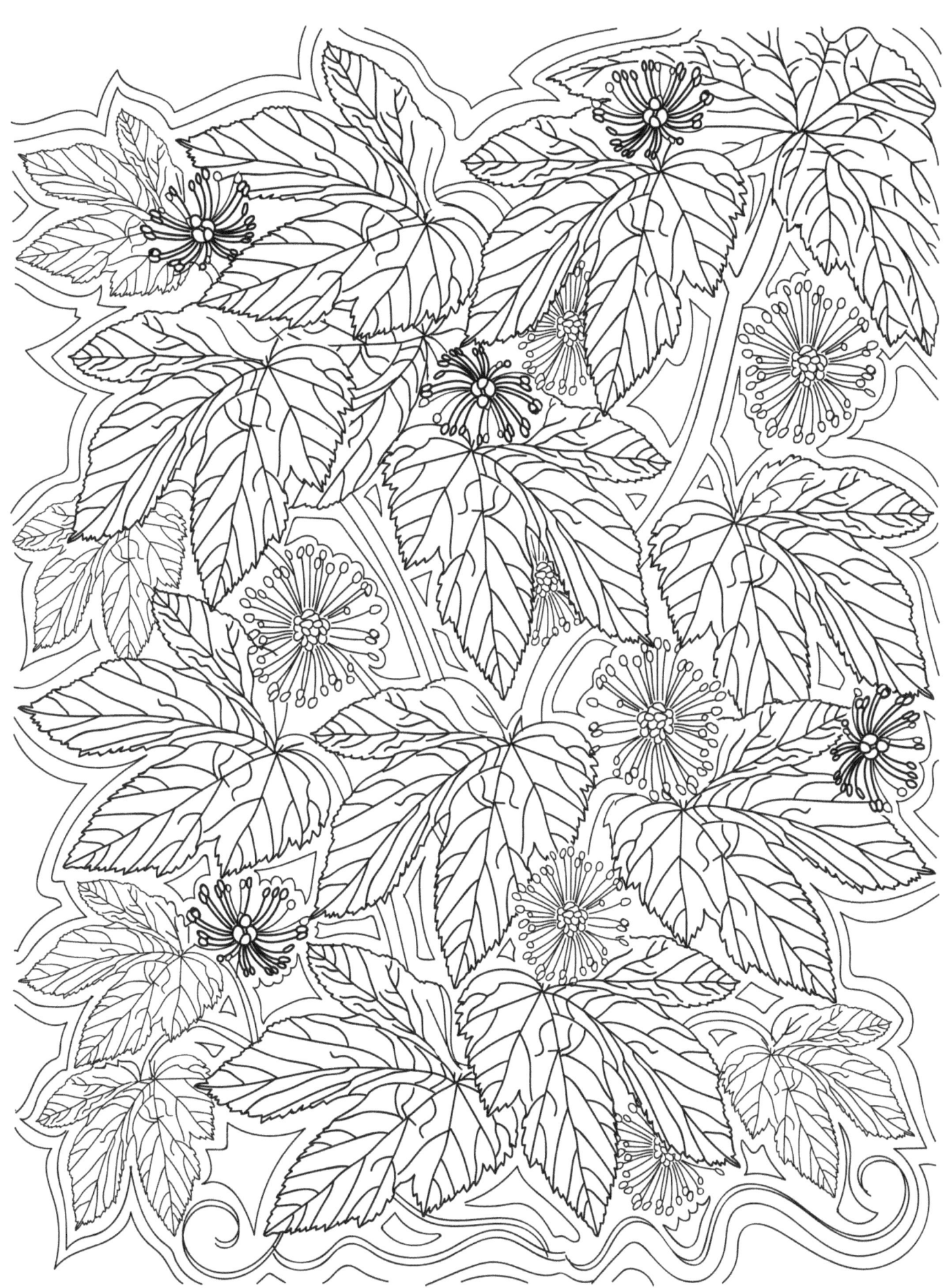

Goldenseal

Artwork By:

Completed On:

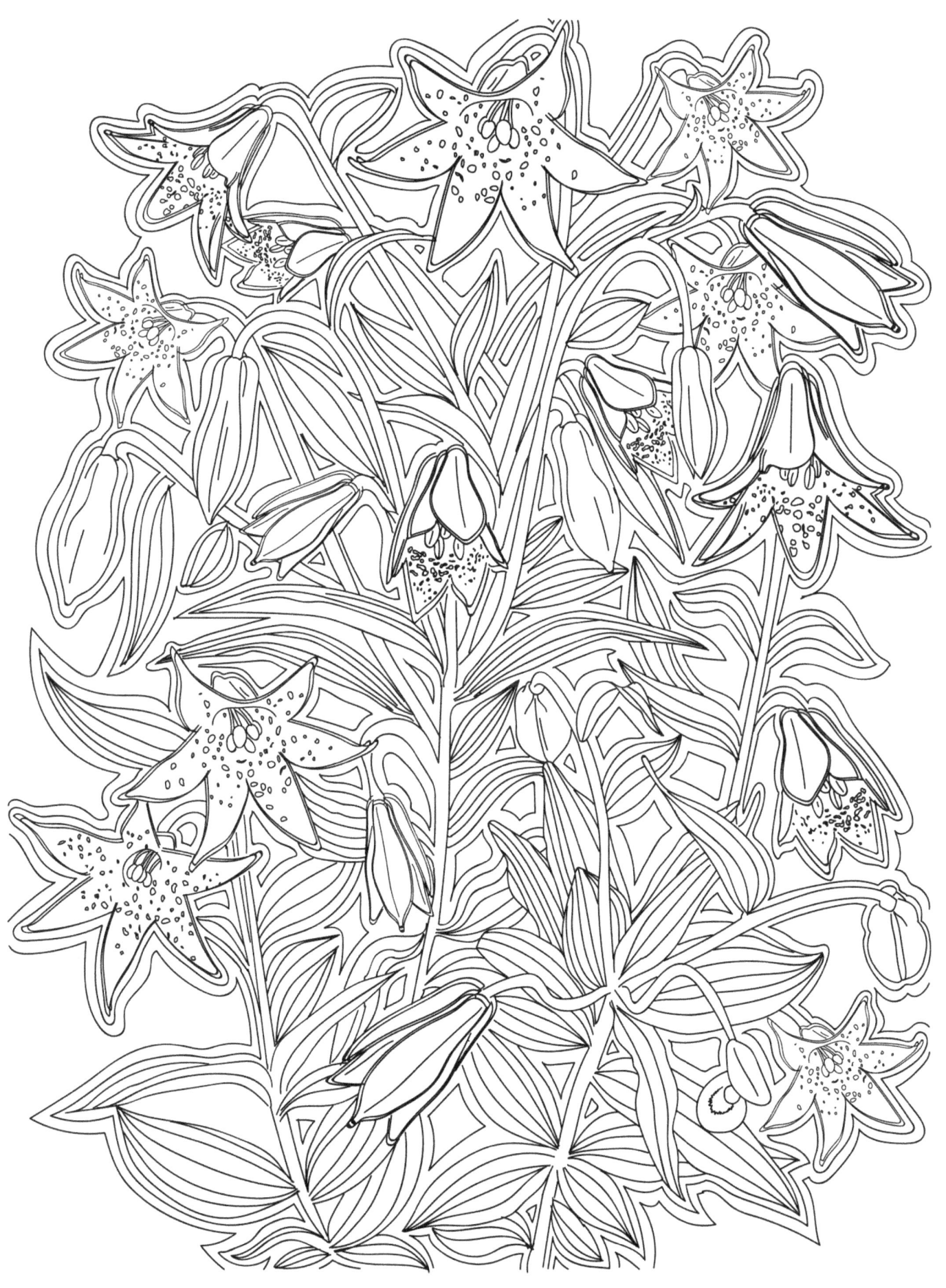

Gray's Lily

Artwork By:

Completed On:

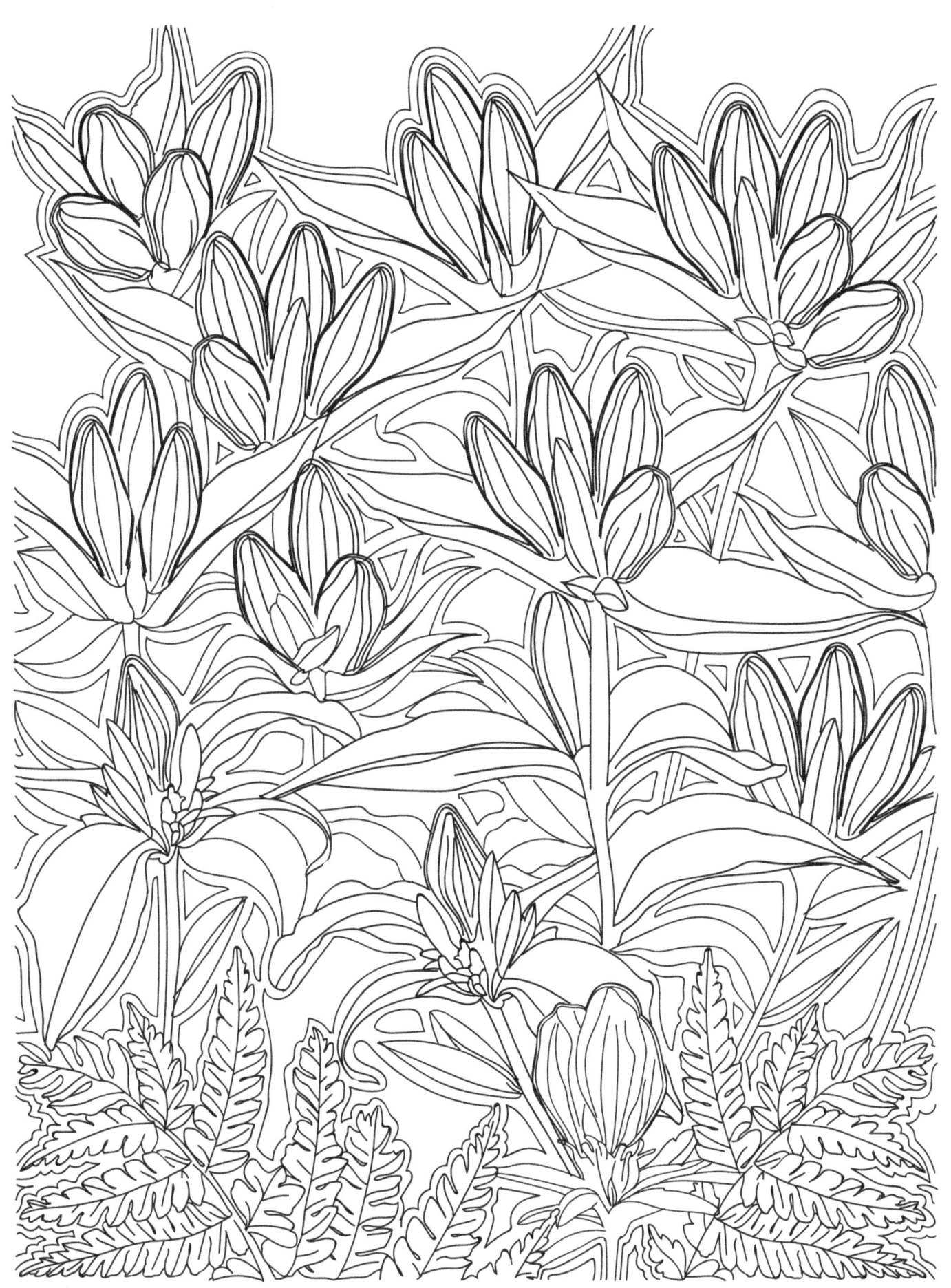

Closed Gentian

Artwork By:

Completed On:

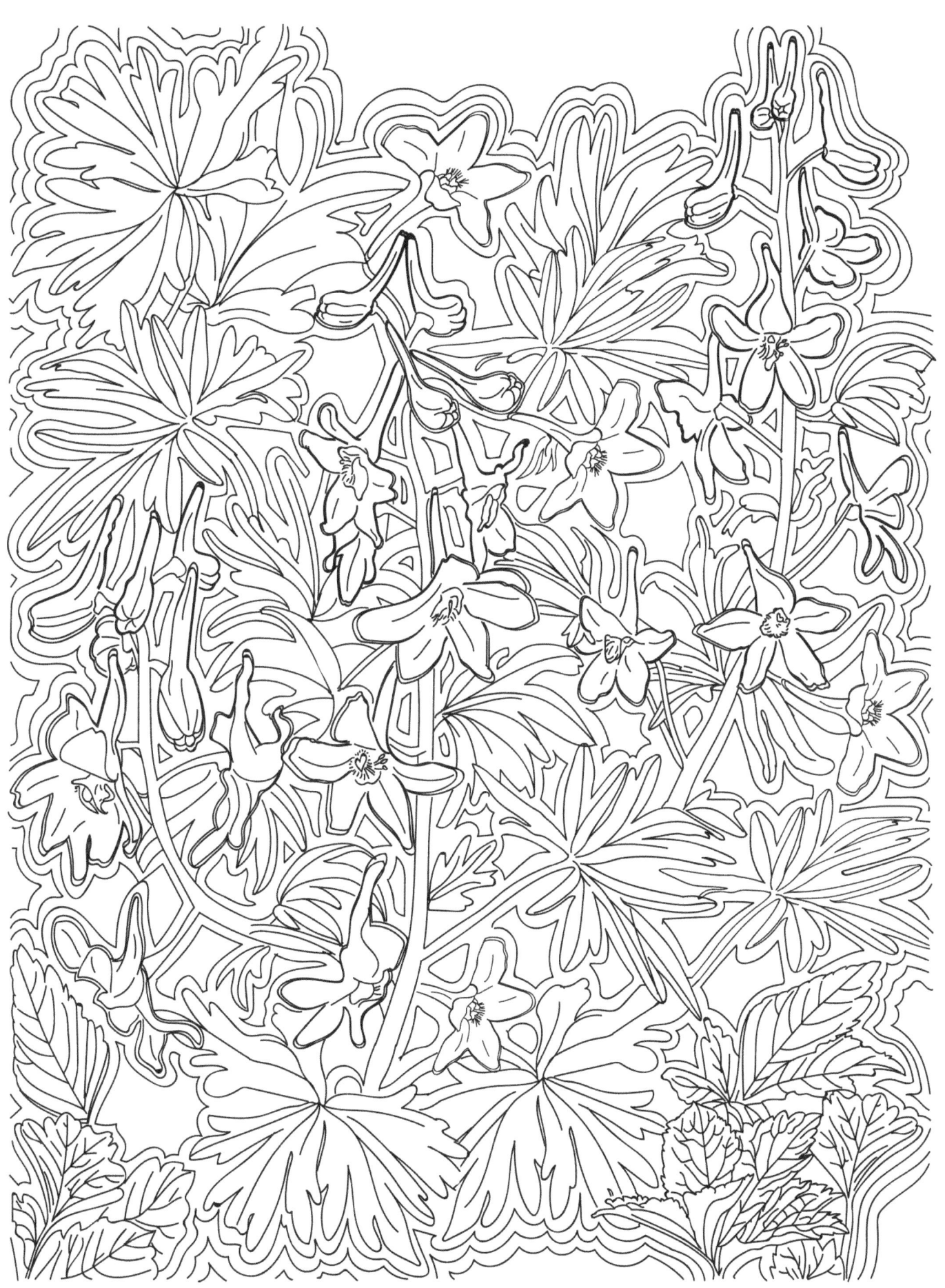

Larkspur

Artwork By:

Completed On:

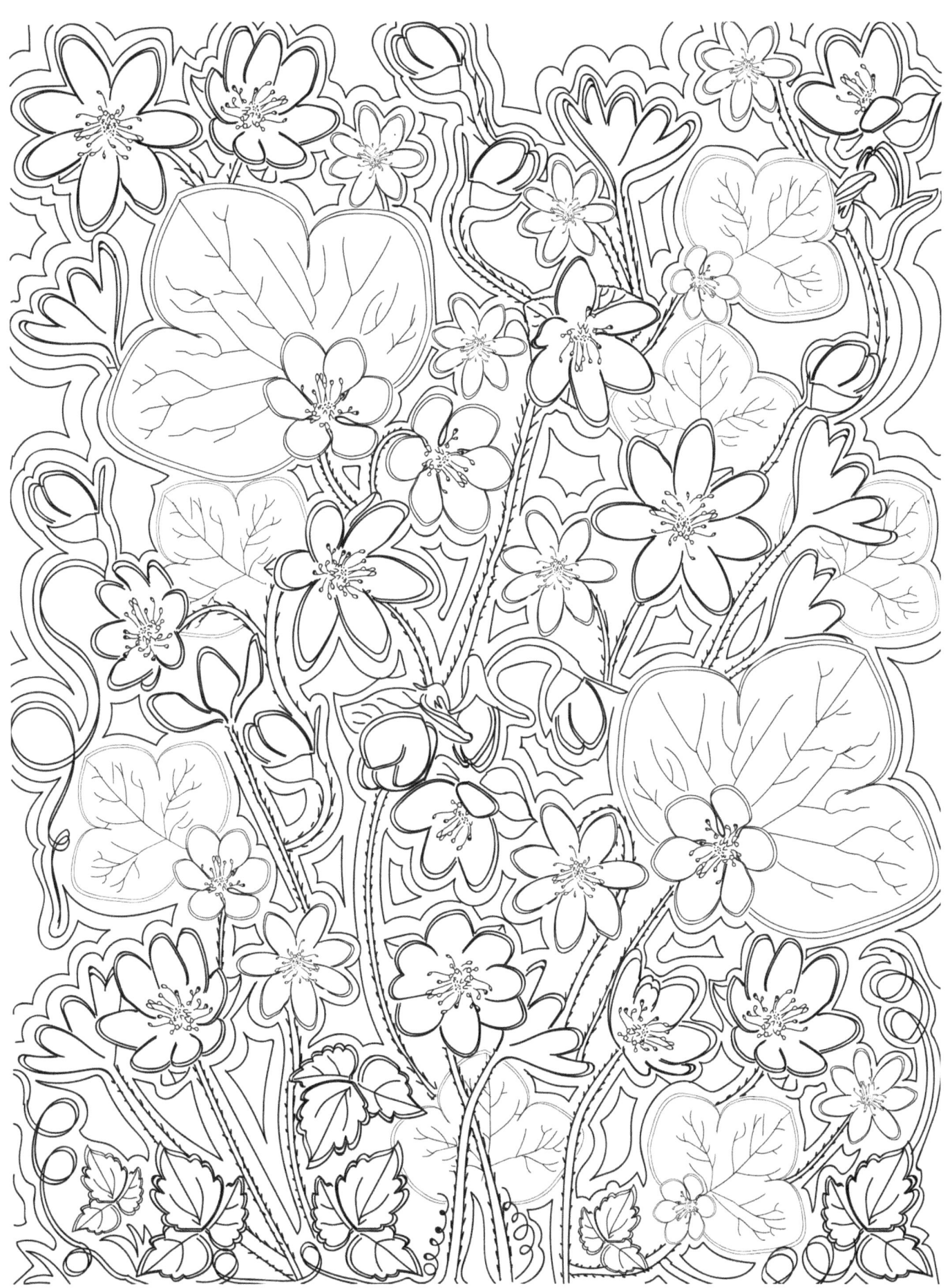

Hepetica

Artwork By:

Completed On:

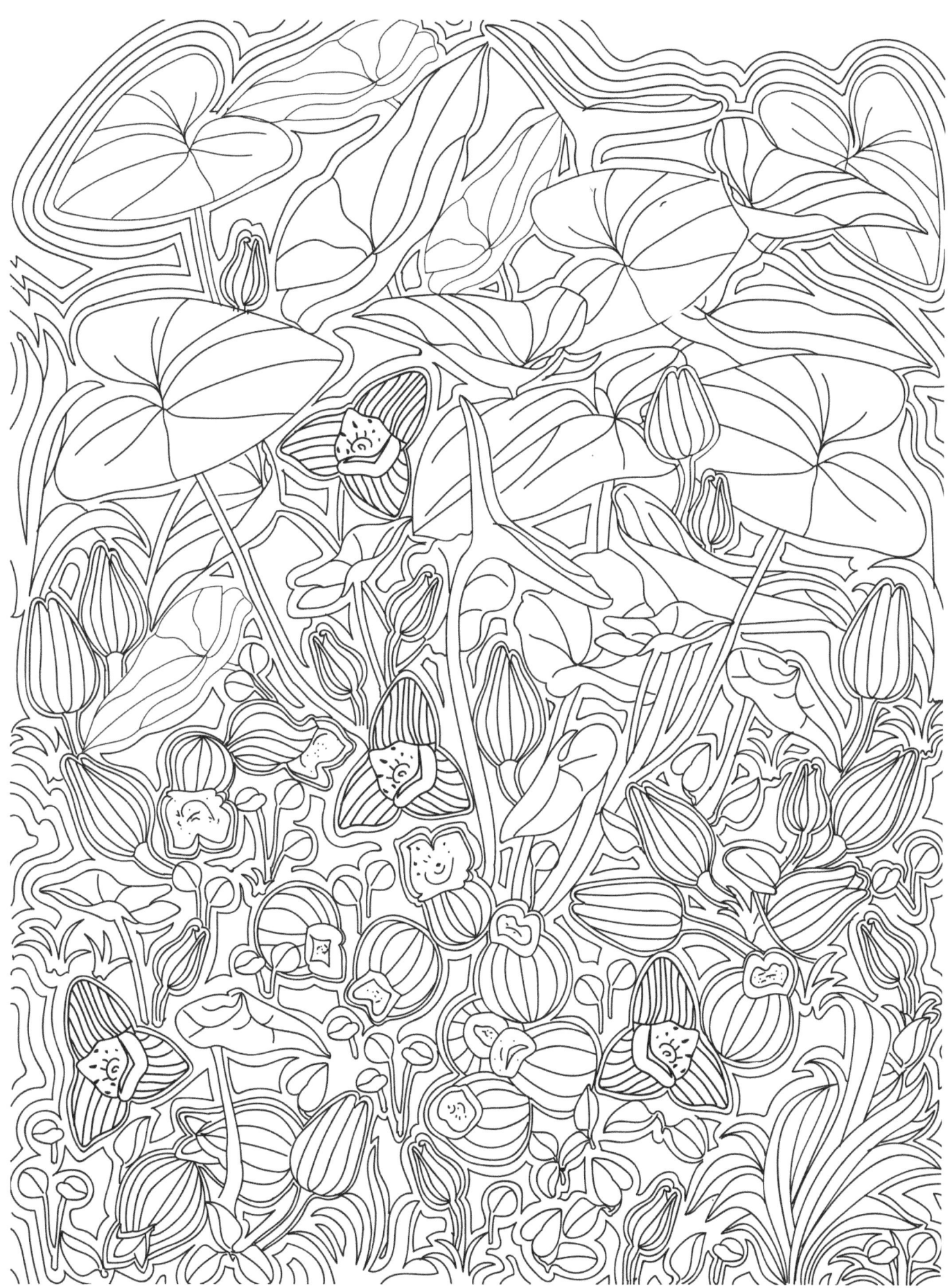

Little Brown Jug

Artwork By:

Completed On:

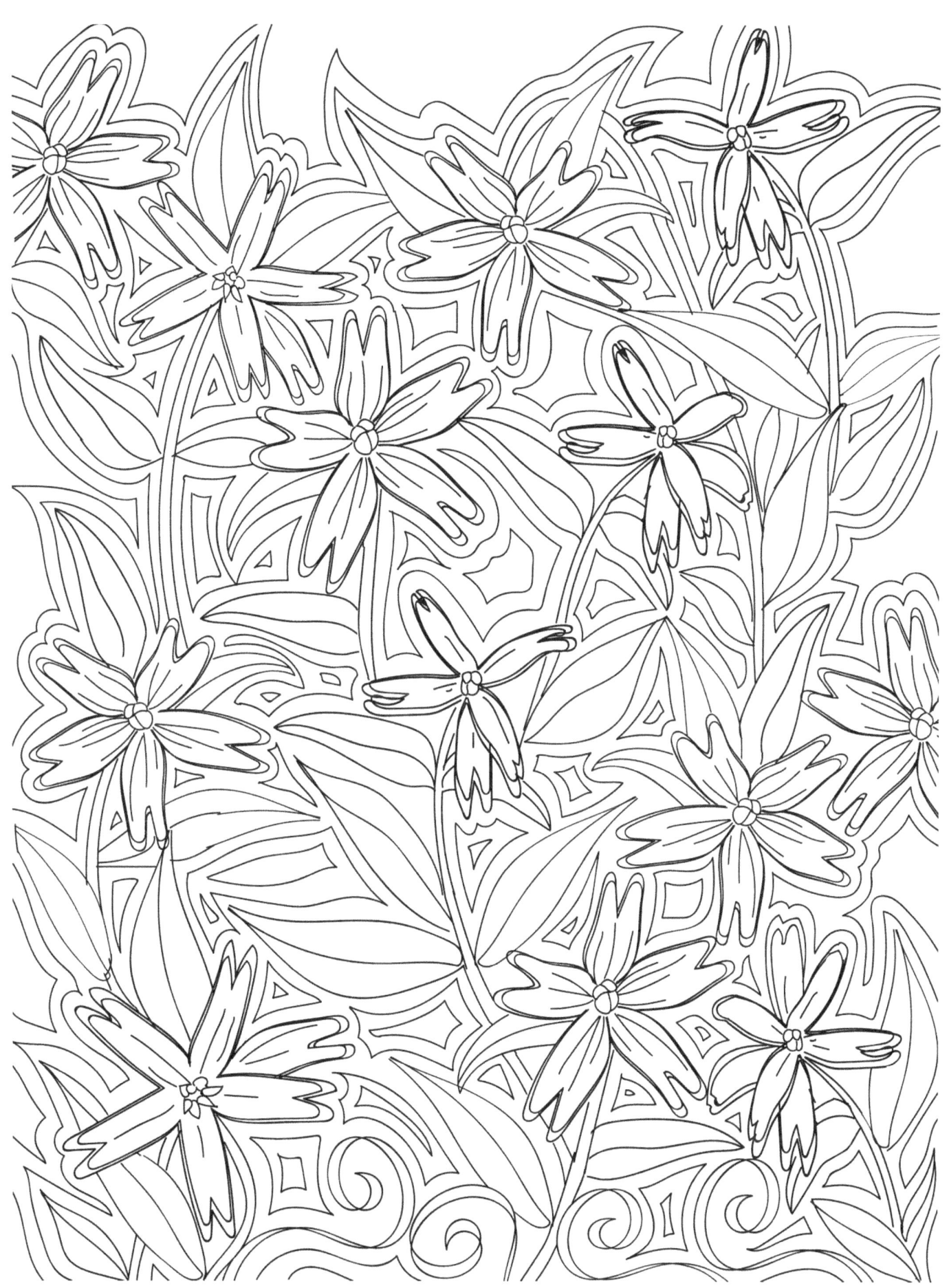

Fire Pink

Artwork By:

Completed On:

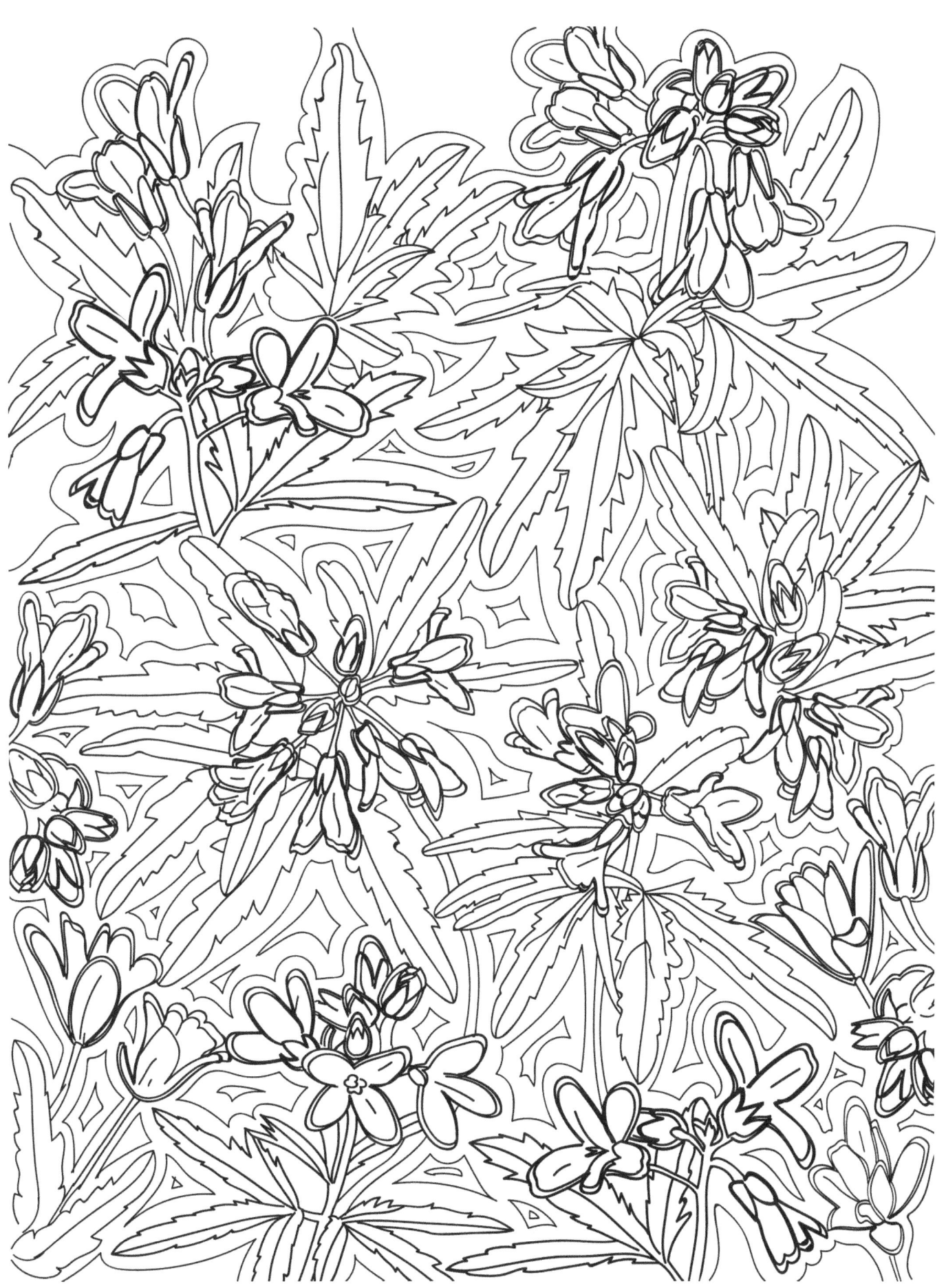

Cut Leaved Toothwort

Artwork By:

Completed On:

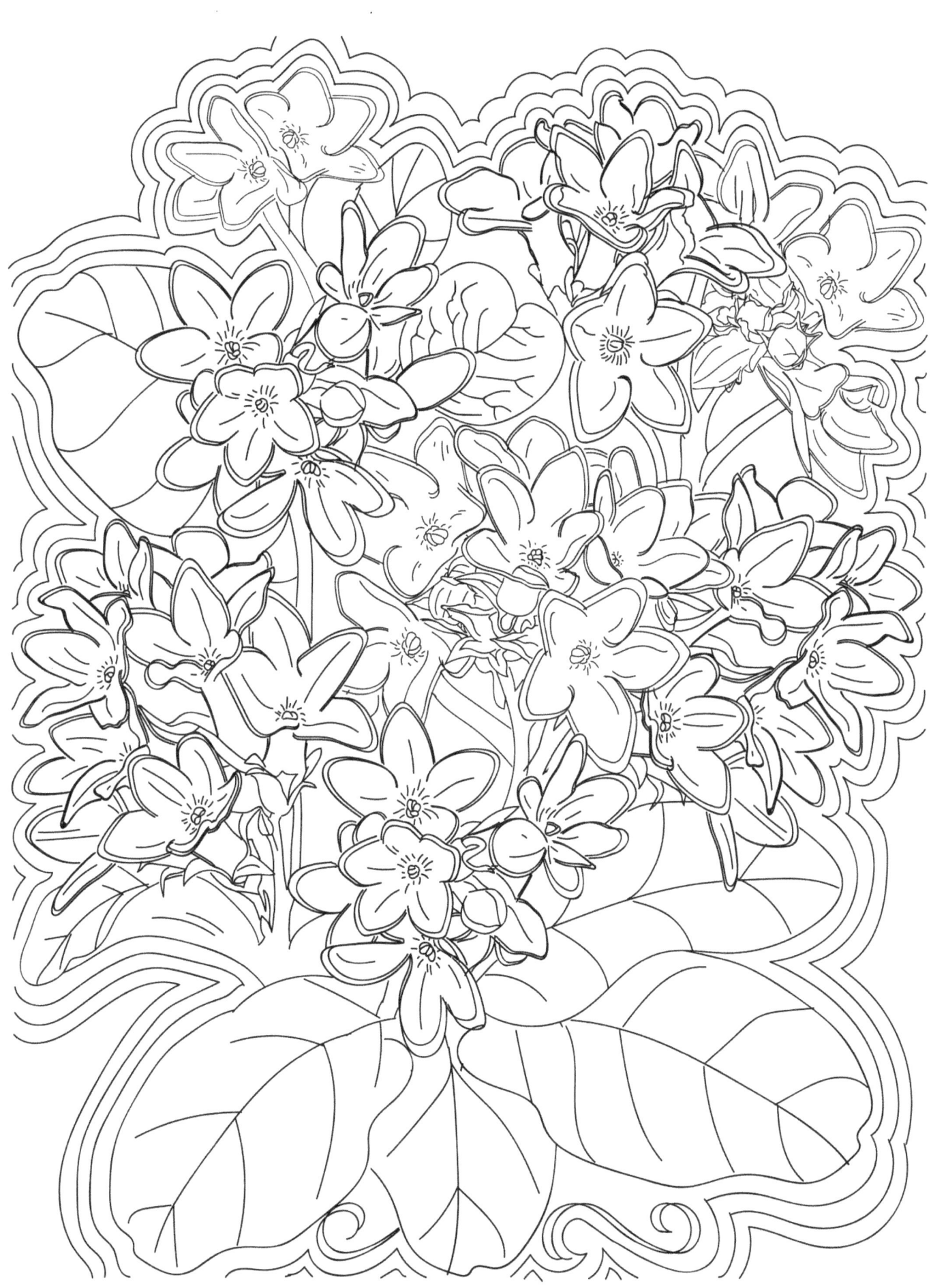

Trailing Arbutus

Artwork By:

Completed On:

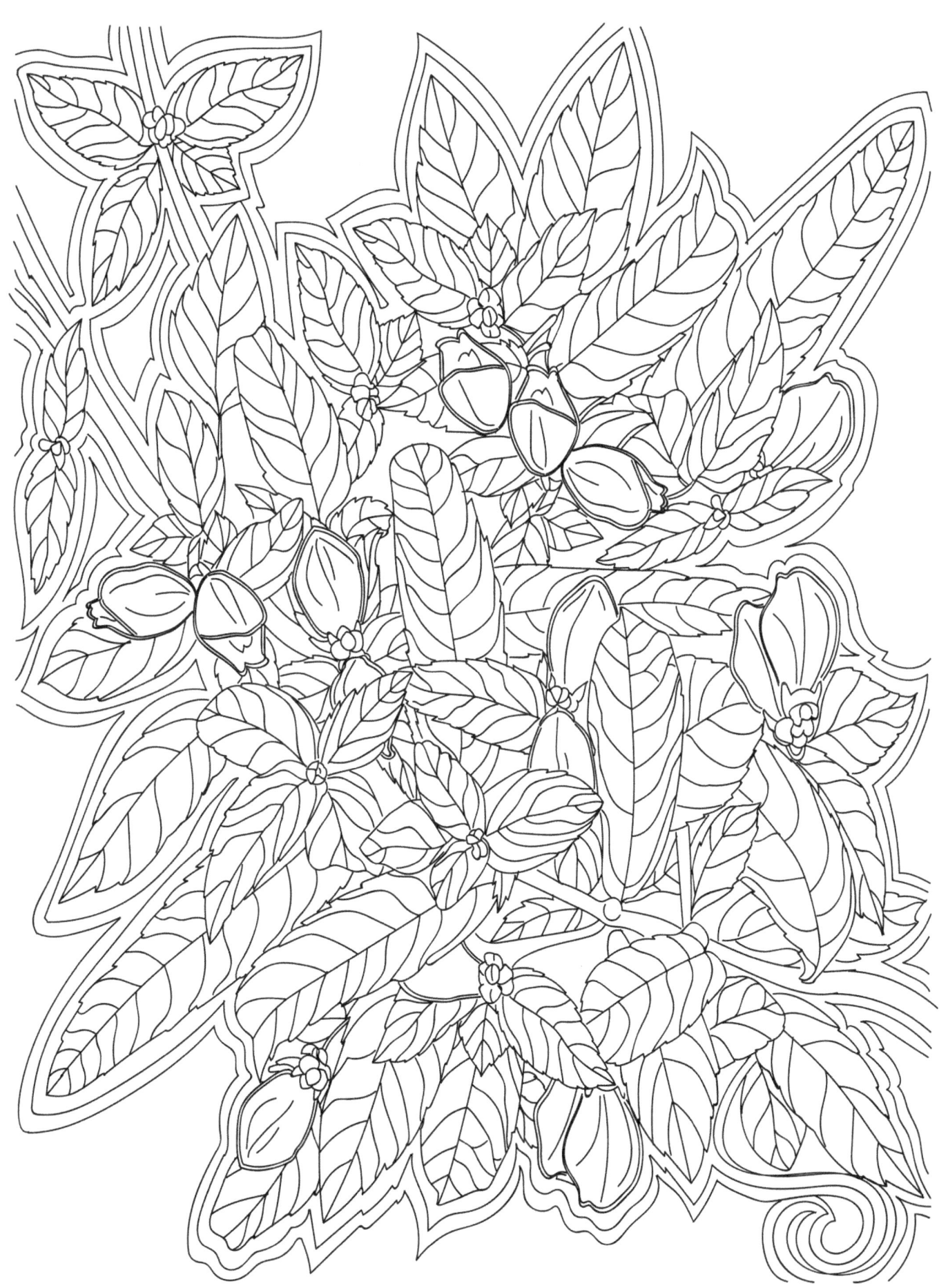

Turtlehead

Artwork By:

Completed On:

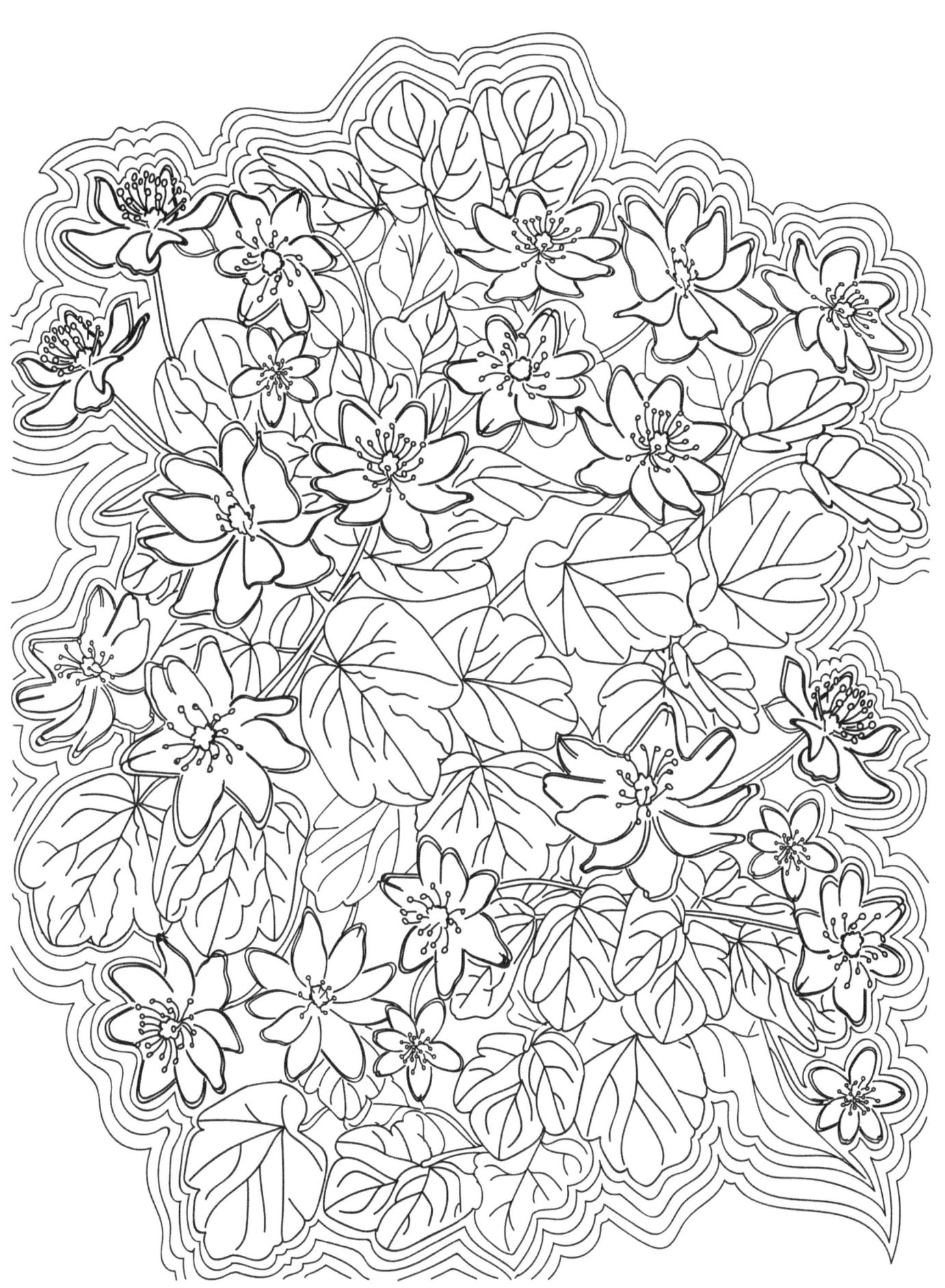

Rue Anemone

Artwork By:

Completed On:

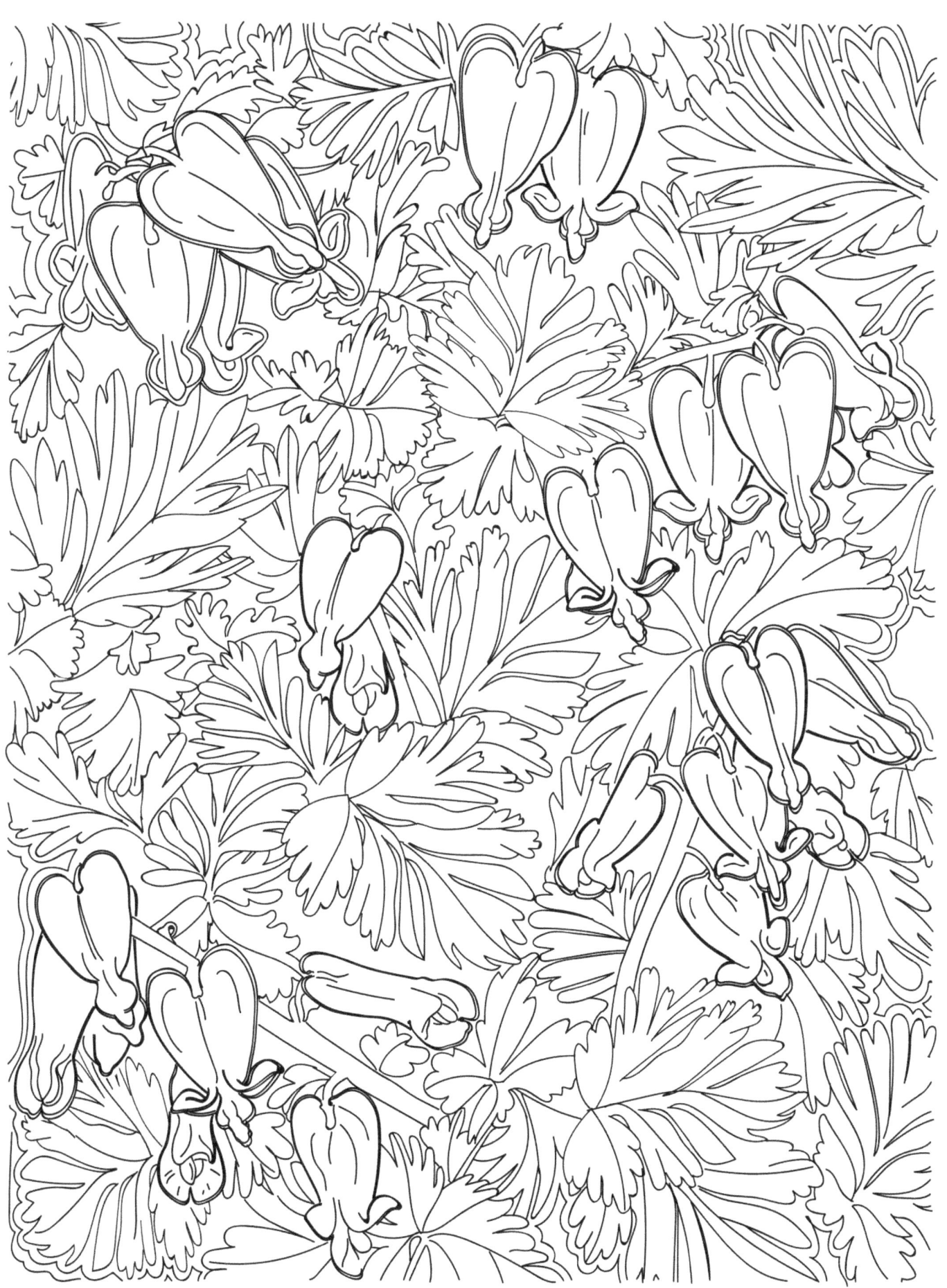

Squirrel Corn

Artwork By:

Completed On:

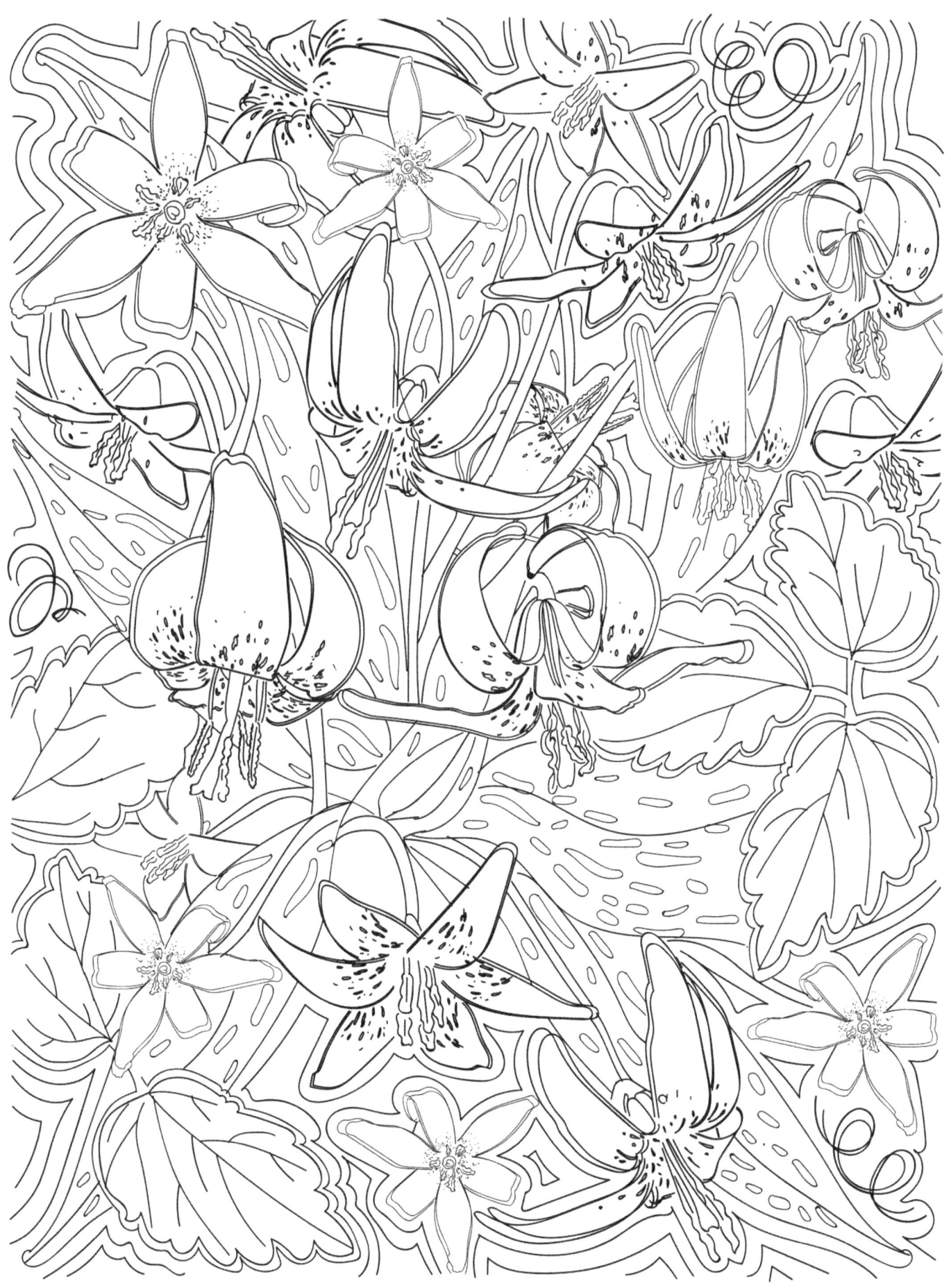

Trout Lily

Artwork By:

Completed On:

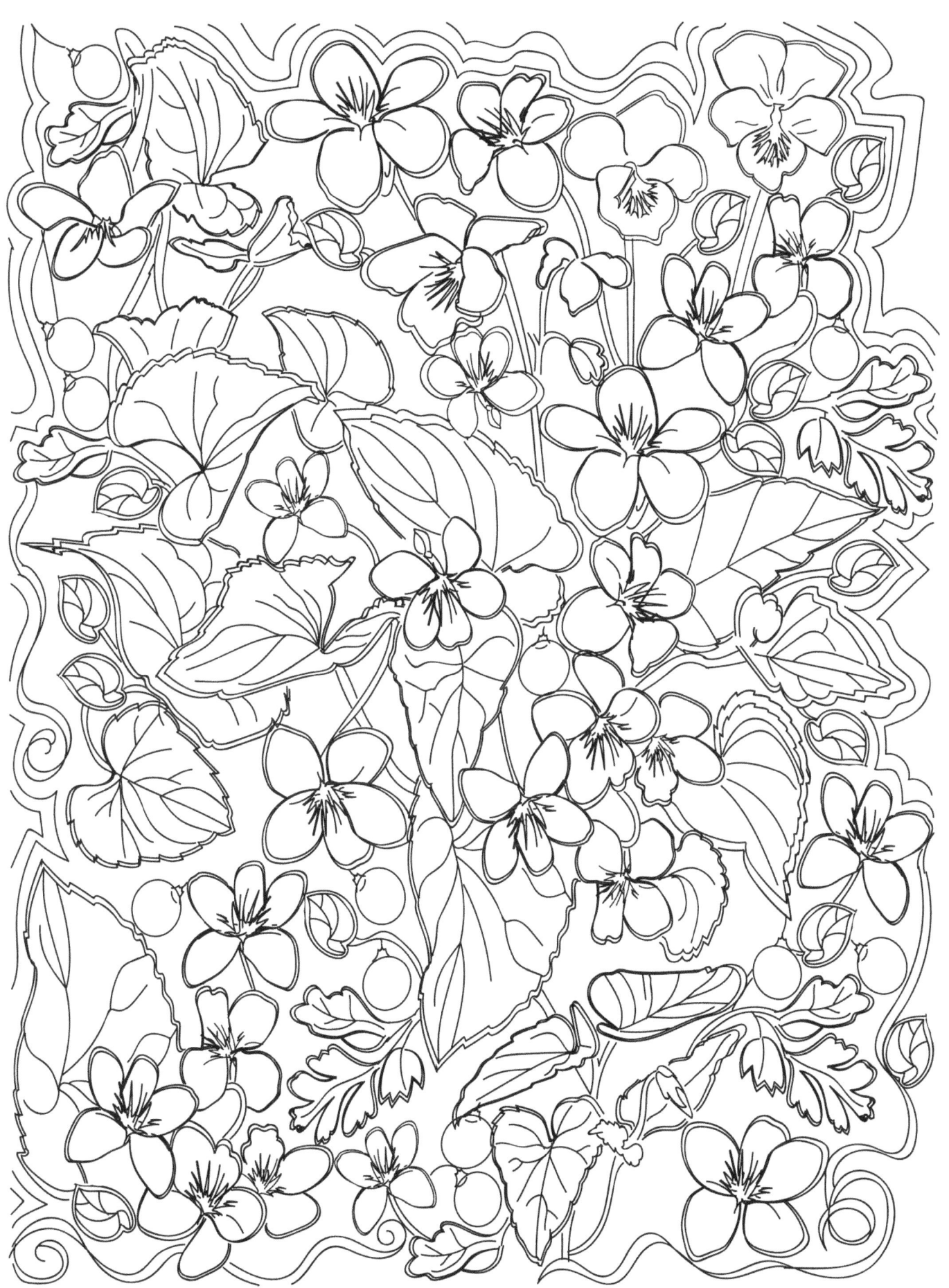

Violet

Artwork By:

Completed On:

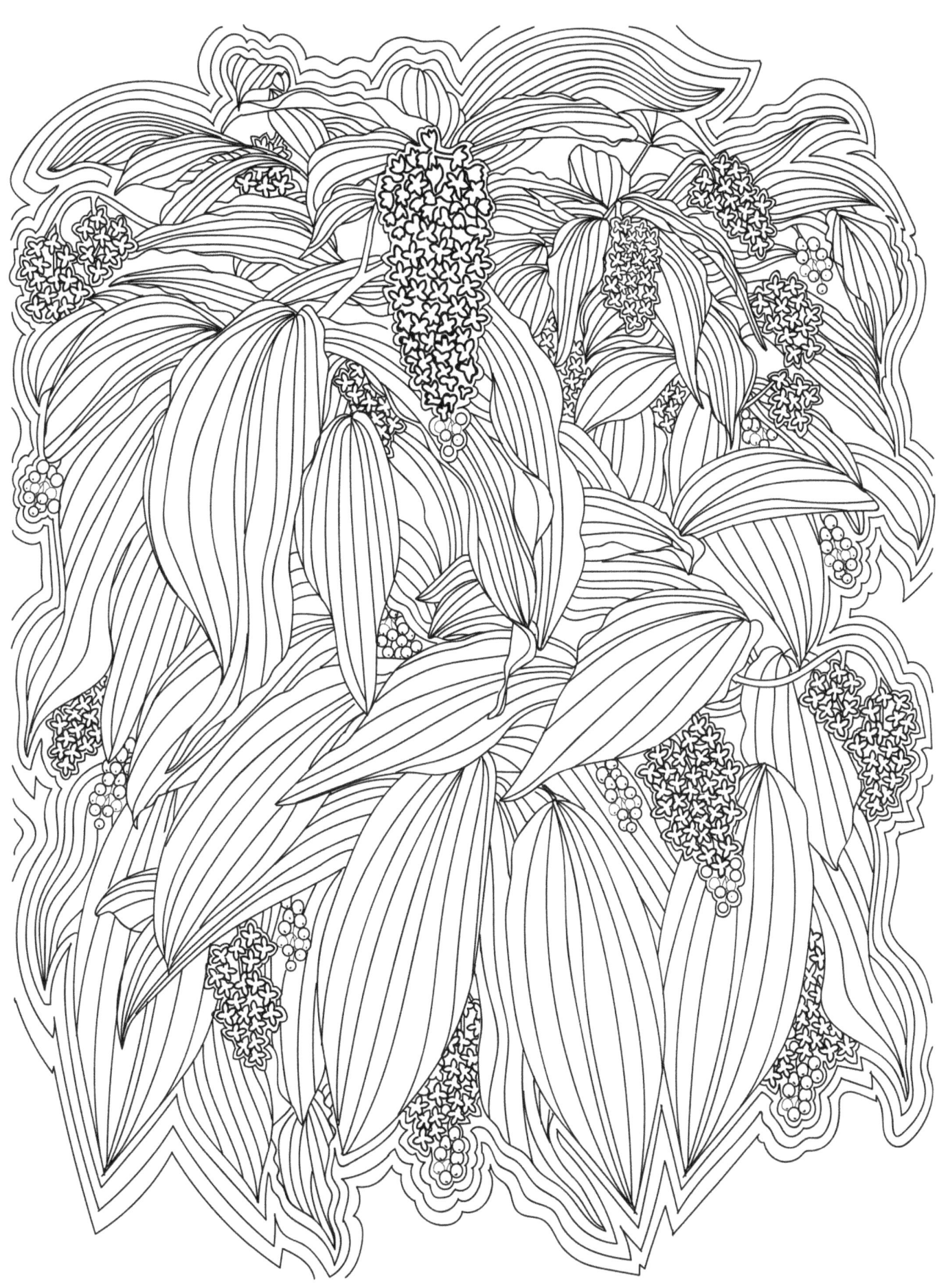

False Solomon's Seal

Artwork By:

Completed On: